FOX FAMILY

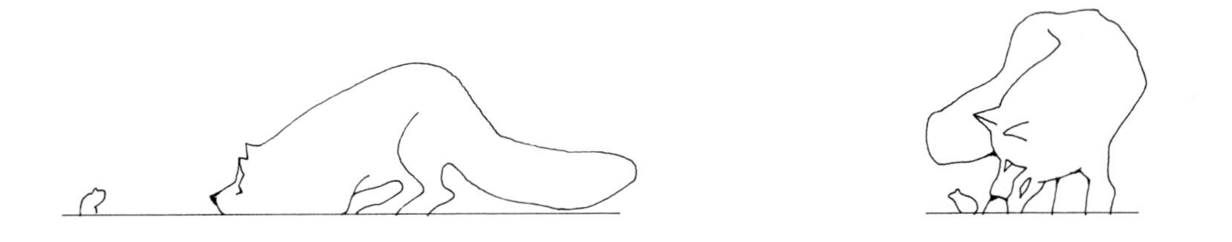

photographs and text by Minoru Taketazu · *translated and adapt*

Richard L. Gage

Fox Family

Four Seasons of Animal Life

New York · WEATHERHILL/HEIBONSHA · *Tokyo*

This book has been adapted for Western readers from two books in Japanese by the same author, both published by Heibonsha: *Kitakitsune* (Northern Fox; 1974) and *Tobe kitakitsune* (Ezo Fox; 1978). Translated and adapted for Western readers by Richard L. Gage.

FIRST EDITION, 1979

Jointly published by John Weatherhill, Inc., of New York and Tokyo, with editorial offices at 7-6-13 Roppongi, Minato-ku, Tokyo 106, Japan, and Heibonsha, of Tokyo.

Library of Congress Cataloging in Publication Data: Gage, Richard L. / Fox family. / Adapted from two works, Kitakitsune hokuhen no gen ya o kakeru and Tobe kitakitsune. / 1. Red fox—Behavior. / 2. Familial behavior in animals. / 3. Mammals—Behavior. / I. Taketazu, Minoru. Kitakitsune hokuhen no gen ya o kakeru. / II. Taketazu, Minoru. Tobe kitakitsune. / III. Title. / QL737.C22G33 / 599'.74442 / 79–9286 / ISBN 0–8348–1039–5

Contents

Introduction

This book is a love lyric relating eight years of adventurous contacts between a veterinarian and the foxes of Hokkaido, the northernmost island in the Japanese archipelago. It begins with the freezing winds from the Sea of Okhotsk sweeping the dunes of the Shiretoko Peninsula and goes on to pursue the always fascinating, frequently mysterious lives of foxes as they survive the cold and breed in the blizzards of winter. In the pale green of spring, they bear young that grow among riots of flowers in the northern summer fields and then, after the severe ceremony of parting between parent and offspring, they go their lonely ways into a new winter.

Our town, Koshimizu, and its surrounding grass plains are located far in the north, where, after descending southward and turning to the east, the Okhotsk coastline of Hokkaido comes together with the Shiretoko Peninsula and then turns westward. To the south is Mount Mokoto; to the east, the odd valleys and peaks of the Shari Range; and to the west, Lake Tōfutsu, a paradise for wild birds. The hilly stretch of shoreline between the lake and the Sea of Okhotsk is a primeval nature preserve. South of the grass plains stretch spacious fields where beets, potatoes, and asparagus are grown among natural windbreaking forests running east and west at intervals of about four kilometers. The blue waters of the Ponyanbetsu River, which has its source on Mount Mokoto, carry many kinds of land and sea creatures into the Okhotsk.

Dim and gloomy even in the daytime, the forests to the south of our town provide places where the Hokkaido bear roams and the giant woodpecker, striped owl, and white-tailed eagle fly. These forests are very much the same today as they were before Hokkaido was colonized. The alluvial fields at the mouth of the Ponyanbetsu encourage cattle breeding. In the summer, the gently rolling hills of the shoreline east and west of the river mouth are flowery fields, like those around Lake Tōfutsu.

About eight hundred meters south of the river mouth is a natural windbreak forest running east and west and about one hundred meters wide. Lake Tōfutsu, the boundary between Koshimizu and Shari, is west of the forest. The small world created by this forest and the shore is a wonderful place for wildlife study. The trees themselves protect the south area from the cruel winds of the sea. People live south of the forest but find the north side incompatible. From the river mouth the seashore stretches to either side in lines unbroken by inlets. The lonely steel of the local one-track train line gleams among grasses along the shore.

I first saw this place in December 1962, when I arrived in Hokkaido to work at a small agricultural veterinary clinic. I had a number of reasons for leaving the warm sun of Kyushu, where I had grown up, for this desolate place, which even the indigenous Ainu consider a kind of *ultima Thule*. First was the dream of a boy from the south to live for a while in a cold climate. The simplicity of the way of life and my longstanding fascination with the local place names too may have played a part in my decision. But, ultimately, the most important reason was my desire to find a new place where I could do something to leave an imprint that showed I had lived. I requested work in Shari, but was sent instead to nearby Koshimizu, where a veterinarian was needed. Though I set out to satisfy the demands of the local people, in practically no time my major interest was captured by the indigenous wildlife. At first word that the swans had come back or that someone had spotted a white-tailed eagle, away I would dash to see it. It is scarcely surprising that the people in charge of the veterinary clinic where I worked abandoned hope of making a good doctor of me. Living proof that a license does not make a veterinarian and responsible for a long list of misdiagnoses, I lived in dread of both my superiors, who wanted to train me to be useful, and the local farmers, who needed my help.

By the time I had somehow or other become a satisfactory animal doctor, I had established a wildlife information network, which, though immensely interesting to me, was totally unrelated to my work. Not everything went as I would have wanted. Once somebody maliciously tossed into my doorway the dead bodies of three black birds of a species declared protected by law in Hokkaido. This shocked and hurt me. Another time I convinced some hunters to take me with them in the hope of seeing a bear. I did spy one, but ran away terrified, like a scared rabbit, leaving behind a camera tripod that had cost an exorbitant sum. Replacing it left me without spending money for months. Furthermore, with my reputation for cowardice, no hunters were ever willing to take me on their expeditions again.

After a number of false starts in the wildlife field, in 1966 I decided to observe foxes regularly. A certain broadcasting company announced the desire to photograph the lives of foxes, and I wanted to cooperate. But, though my information network soon discovered more than forty-four fox dens and families, my friends refused to take my new enthusiasm seriously, especially after the bear-viewing escapade. One of the old Japanese folk traditions about foxes is that they can enchant human beings. Many of the local dairy farmers were convinced that such would be my fate if I continued with the project. Maybe they were right. In the following eight years I observed and spent much time with fox families from over one hundred dens. Today some people still give me a wide berth, for they consider the very length of my investigation of the animals proof positive that the foxes have bewitched me.

In a sense this is true, for my years of association with these creatures have only increased my fascination and love for them. Watching fox families breed and rear their young and then disperse when the cubs reach maturity, I have gained a greater appreciation both of these small, beautiful animals and of nature as a whole. I have also increasingly realized the harm and destruction that man continues to inflict on wildlife as he infringes upon nature in his desire to build and develop. What I present here is a record of fox family life to share and enjoy with the reader. Hopefully he too will be bewitched by these fascinating creatures.

Fox Family: An Essay

WINTER The flowering plants that brought pleasure to tourists in summer are locked in cold earth, awaiting spring. Silence reigns in the north, and the Sea of Okhotsk is covered by apparently endless ice floes. The Ponyanbetsu River too is ice-capped and still. Forests and fields lie under white snow that the winds have swirled into miniature replicas of waves. Smoke rising from chimneys indicates that human beings are active as they await the spring. But outdoors the blizzard, driven by the north wind, moves across a world where all appears dead.

Then through the driving snow and across the ice floes flashes a streak of red-gold. A flame-colored life against dead white. A creature with white breast thrust boldly into the wind and ears resolutely pinned back. A fox abroad because the frozen world of February is the backdrop for vulpine amours.

My observations began in February with tracks that tell the observant eye a great deal. First, they show that if some foxes travel far afield, others operate in surprisingly limited zones. Some invariably visit abandoned hunters' shacks or local dairy farms in search of food. Others rarely go to the same place twice. In winter the foxes prefer the artificially forested stands of red pine and natural windbreak forests over the grass plains. When times are hard, foxes begin to eat beets and sweetbrier, which they scorn when live animal food is available.

In the winter of 1971 I spent a great deal of time observing and following a beautiful red vixen who had a small zone of operation—one that she, like other foxes, marked off with droppings and little yellow urine stains in the snow—along the beach in the vicinity of the mouth of the Ponyanbetsu. I enjoyed watching her, and she got used to me. I called her Muni.

After the tenth of the month I noticed tracks of another fox in Muni's zone, but these occurred only once. Two days later I came to the conclusion that Muni had lost her hunting skill, for the number of times she caught prey dropped to zero. At the same time, the urine stains in her zone increased and appeared in higher places than usual. Since the weather was severe, I left food where she could find it. Although from her tracks I knew she was aware of the food, not only did she pay no attention to its attractions, but also one day she shocked me by urinating on a piece of meat that I had left for her.

It turned out, however, that this strange lack of interest in food indicated the initiation of a love affair. The color of the urine stains altered on the tenth day of my observation. And, on the evening of the same day, I saw her walking on the ice at the river mouth and acting rather shy as she was being followed by three male foxes—one directly behind her, one about twenty meters farther back, and the last about fifty meters to the rear and to the right. In spite of the way in which she seemed to ignore them, the males, ears and tails tense, followed her step by step.

When Muni disappeared over the top of one of the white-covered dunes east of the river mouth, the second male fox suddenly darted forward for a few meters, raising a cloud of powdery snow. Then the first one flew forward with a sharp barking sound. The second darted back again, yapping as he came. Then the third joined in the din. Ears pinned back, tails pulled slightly between their legs, they barked at the red setting sun, while, a few seconds later, the indifferent Muni bounded out of sight over another dune. This drove the males to start after her, carefully keeping their proper intervals. I knew then that Muni's mating was only a few hours away.

In early April, Muni's tracks in the remaining snow no longer made a straight line, but veered first right, then left. The babies in her womb were growing heavier. The thaw is a busy time here as the north begins to awaken. Birds who have spent the winter in the south start to return. Frogs creak like rusty pulleys as they splash in pools left by the melting snow. Flowering plants begin to push their way up through softened ground. Especially typical of this part of the world are the pale callalike flowers of the water plaintain, rising from cold, swampy ponds.

At about this time of year, our wild-animal research center is flooded with information, especially about Hokkaido foxes. During winter, the animals stay out of the way of humans as much as possible. But in the spring, what with a scarcity of such prey as field mice and with the need to nourish newborn cubs, vixens are forced to push their search for food much closer to the dwellings of man.

The Hokkaido vixen comes into heat in February and bears cubs in late March or early April. During pregnancy, vixens are extremely wary and nervous. At the slightest indication of danger, they will move their dens. Sometimes, when harm is in the offing, they have been known to eat their own newly born cubs. In the year I am discussing, I resumed observations when information and sightings of foxes began to reach our center in early spring, but, because it was birth season, stayed away from the dens as much as possible.

Some friends who are interested in foxes and I are especially careful on this point, for changes in the environment are reducing the area within which the animals can bear and raise their young in security. A number of years ago it was possible for vixens to make dens over a wide zone in the grass plains near our village, but all that has changed now. For instance, in the past, tourists never appeared in this part of the island until July, when the wildflowers are at their peak; by that time vixens were already at their ease since their cubs had grown strong and active. Not long ago, however, as the Japanese National Railway electrified its lines and discontinued use of old steam locomotives, steam-engine fans traveled far and wide to photograph the few remaining ones that continued in operation on Hokkaido. As it turned out, the train line running along the beach from near the mouth of the Ponyanbetsu used steam locomotives. Over a number of years, these buffs came to our village throughout the year in large numbers to photograph the trains. This wrought havoc on the foxes breeding places. In one field where I had previously observed six families, there were only two in the following year. And the year after that, there were none.

But, as information we gathered shows, foxes prove amazingly tolerant and resourceful in selection of other—often highly unlikely—places to bear their young. In one field stands an abandoned house around which observers have reported seeing cubs at play. Some vixens and their young have enough fortitude to live in culverts under roads and to remain calm when cars and trucks roar overhead. One farmer told of the hilarious fun he had watching fox cubs playing with piglets from the pens next to which their vixen mother had found a home under a fallen tree. Some vixens even make dens among the refuse heaps of the town dump, where they can command a rich, varied menu including all kinds of tempting delicacies abandoned by human beings. I suspect the cubs born in such locales are the epicures of the Hokkaido fox world.

But the happiest cubs are the ones—like those of my Muni—born among the dunes at the sea edge, where their first glimpse of the outside world is a of a golden dandelion carpet on the sand and the mountains of the Shiretoko Peninsula soaring in the distance.

SPRING When the strong southern winds characteristic of this region in late April begin to raise the temperatures, I find myself incapable of remaining calmly at home. I know the cubs are beginning to play around the mouth of the den. The more cubs there are in a litter, the sooner they emerge from the hole. I can imagine the constant bickering that must take place in an especially crowded fox home.

In 1969 I was observing a vixen, whom I called Tōhachi and who, like Muni, had a lair in the seaside dunes. Tōhachi was a worker, and she had to labor all the harder because her mate practically never returned to the den. But she had a friend in Mr. Sekine, who owned a pig farm where Tōhachi often visited. Mr. Sekine frequently gave her table scraps or even a piglet that had died for some reason or other. I did not see Tōhachi after winter observations until May 14, when the strong southern winds were blowing.

As usual, I was happy at the prospect of meeting the foxes again, but I was wary too. I had not seen the mother for over two months. Would she tolerate my presence? If she or her mate barked in the characteristic high, warning fashion that I had come to know, things would be difficult. How could I put them at their ease so that they would allow my observations?

After considerable thought, I decided to become a popular singer—that is, instead of sneaking quietly up on them in the hope of preserving their calm, I decided to sing out loud from a long way off so that they would know I was coming and could take whatever precautionary steps they thought necessary. I adopted as my singing model a young male vocalist who was popular at the time and of whom I myself was fond.

On the following morning, I—the new singing rage—set out. As I approached the small hill not far from Tōhachi's den, I was disappointed to hear the sharp warning bark I had feared. Still I crooned the sentimental lyrics of a love song as I approached to a distance of about fifty meters from the den entrance. All was quiet. Peace in front of the den. Success!

The den had been enlarged since I last saw it in March, and a low mound of sand around the entrance told of the work that had gone into the expansion project. Over the surface of the sand were small, mischievous tracks, like those of kittens. I took up my post on a small hill overlooking the den mouth from a distance of about fifty meters.

Tōhachi had four cubs—not a large family, not a small one. In some cases vixens bear as many as seven or as few as two. Fox cubs are dark brown at birth; red hair only begins to appear after thirty days or so. At the time of my initial observations, Tohachi's babies were about fifty days old.

In front of the den hole sat a cub, a ball of dark brown fur, with a pencil-size tail, barely white-tipped at its one end, and a little face, very different from the sharp, foxy look of faces of adults, at its other. Between two leaf-shaped ears was a rounded forehead and a tiny button nose. By no stretch of the imagination could the eyes be called penetrating and clear. They were more like slightly clouded, blue-black marbles. Not yet used to walking, when the little creature put forth a foot and found under it a piece of ground different from what it had expected, down it tumbled. The joints apparently refused to perform as they should, and the cub wobbled clownishly.

In the habit of giving names to the foxes I observed, I soon found appellations for these on the basis of their characteristics: Whitey, Red, and Blackie, for obvious reasons. But for a while, I was unable to decide on a name that expressed the distinctive traits of the fourth. Then I noticed that he dashed terrified into the lair at my slightest movement. He clearly did not like me. For this reason, I called him Hysterics, a name I have used for other fox cubs who showed pronounced aversions to me.

Tōhachi's hunting day began at about three and ended around five, when she returned with her prey, usually a few mice, or sometimes birds or even dead fish. As she approached the den with food, she invariably made a clucking sound that brought the heretofore sleeping cubs bounding forth. This call undoubtedly meant something like "Come and get it!" No matter what the size of the prey or the number of pieces involved, it belongs to the cub who snaps it up first. A strict law of first come, first served prevails, and even the strongest cubs find it difficult to take away that which they have been too late to claim. This system is to the advantage of the weak cubs, who can keep their ears tuned for the parent's call, even from a distance, and dash out of the lair first. The ones who miss out on the prey rush headlong for mother's teats. Tōhachi stands, and the three cubs, rearing up on their hind paws, massage her breasts until the milk spurts forth. Then, ceasing the massaging motion, they nurse with a sucking sound for from three to five minutes. Depending on the number of cubs and the condition of the mother, the length of time varies. I have observed cubs who nursed for as long as sixteen minutes. Since she is standing, Tōhachi is able to keep her eyes on the lookout for danger from all directions and can dash to safety if need arises.

Generally, after playing with the cubs for a little while, Tōhachi went out hunting again. After about seven-thirty in the morning her activity slacked, ceasing entirely between eight and noon, when she was never to be seen. Often she returned from her first afternoon hunting foray with nothing, and I assumed that the reason for her trip home at that hour was to give the cubs a chance to nurse. After three, she frequently returned with prey, and her hunting activities came to a close at about seven in the evening. Tōhachi's punctuality in these matters may have been the result of her own personality or may have been related to the diurnal schedules of field mice, her primary quarry.

In early June, the Sea of Okhotsk wears its most peaceful face. Salmon begin to run up the Ponyanbetsu, and the fields are a tapestry of golden dandelions and nodding black lilies. The birds begin to build nests in the new green of the windbreak forests, and everywhere the slightly lazy calm of spring lingers.

Everywhere, that is, except in fox dens, where war is being

waged. Even with the help of the male, who must spend much of his time on guard duty, the vixen is engaged in a grueling battle with the bellies of her cubs.

From my vantage point in front of the den I could tell not only the cruel demands the cubs made on their parents—who seemed to go without food and sleep—but also the mélange of things the parents dragged home to appease their offspring's appetites. Of course, there were the purely natural things that they were able to capture in hunting: field mice, birds, fish, squirrels, and baby hares. But in addition they occasionally amplified the menu with piglets, chickens, dried fish, salt trout, sheepskins, pickled octopus, a strong pickle made of the *daikon* radish, cabbages weighing as much as a kilogram, and even a can of mixed spices. In my mind, I conjured up the fox dinner: roast mouse, fillet of breast of chicken, and piquant cabbage salad. At first I was surprised to notice the large percentage of cow and pig afterbirths in the food the vixen brought home. On second thought, however, I realized that this was not surprising since in our town there are about four thousand milk cows and a thousand brood sows. These animals probably produce enough afterbirths in a year to feed more than a hundred foxes. In this respect, the feeding habits of the foxes I observed bore an interesting similarity to the habits of the canine animals in the African savannah that adjust their movements according to the breeding of the gnu and other animals.

But even on this rich diet, the cubs gave their parents no rest. One day I followed Muni on a hunting trip. At the time, she was rearing five ravenous cubs. The course she followed was slightly different from the one to which she had been accustomed in winter and seemed a little capricious. Still she was completely absorbed in what she was doing and concentrated on perceiving all sounds made around her. I tried to stay to the hillocks and ridges from which I could observe her better. Walking a while, then stopping, then going on, she preferred the hollows and ravines, and was especially careful in searching through dense undergrowth.

Once as she was walking along the bank of the Ponyanbetsu, she stopped suddenly, tensed her ears, and crouched slightly. Then, once again, she displayed the incredible grace of her hunting leap. Her body a golden whiplash, she dancingly flew straight up and then fell on her prey, using her front paws and muzzle to seize it and her hind legs to prevent its escape. But this practically soundless performance was much less effective than it was beautiful. Sometimes she had to repeat her leap as many as fourteen times to catch one field mouse, and at other times, even after all this effort, she lost her game. On one occasion I observed her take a bird this way, though actually she had little reason to use the leap on flying creatures, for, once she jumps and startles, they fly away. And she doesn't get a second chance at them. With one catch in her mouth, she continued hunting. (I have heard claims that foxes sometimes hunt in pairs. Since I have never observed them doing so, I cannot say.) On the day I followed her, Muni hunted without pause for an hour and a half and caught only two field mice.

As I have already suggested, Muni and other Hokkaido foxes depend on their sense of hearing when hunting. Since wind and rain drown out sounds, the weather plays a determining role in the kind of food that foxes take home to their young. On calm, fine days, natural prey accounts for seventy percent of the total, but when the wind is strong or when rain falls, eighty percent is refuse or food that is in one way or another connected with man and his activities. Furthermore, on such bad days, hunting goes on at a slack pace all day without the morning and evening breaks usual on fair-weather days. (Incidentally, a friend of mine doing research on rodents says that wind and rain have little effect on the diurnal habits of field mice.)

Foxes have very poor eyesight. Inexperienced cubs are especially shortsighted and cannot differentiate things at a distance of more than fifty paces. I have seen Muni's cubs run in fright from the shadow of a crow flying overhead or dash for cover when I stood up to urinate, though they had already become accustomed to me. Once, mistaking it for one of their parents, they ran hungrily up to a wild dog that was on the verge of attacking them. The dog seemed as surprised by their welcome as they were to discover their error. I chased the startled dog away.

It would seem that, in the well-regulated natural world, selection would long ago have eliminated creatures with as serious a failing as this, but such has not been the case. Whether I have been of use in the improvement of the fox race in general by saving cubs from danger incurred by poor eyesight is a moot point. Adult foxes see a little better, but not much. I estimate that they cannot make accurate distinctions at distances of more than eighty meters.

Once I did some work to assist Professor Hisashi Abe, of Hokkaido University, in experiments on fox olfactory abilities. We learned that a fox is able to detect meat buried in the ground to a depth of up to, but no more than, thirty centimeters, indicating a well-developed sense of smell. Nonetheless, the kinds of animals the fox generally catches clearly lead to the conclusion that hearing is by far their most important hunting sense. To some extent, however, particular predilections under particular circumstances play an important role. I believe that the Hokkaido fox hunts first by sound. When something happens to impair hearing or drown out surrounding noises, the nose comes into play, while the eyes are virtually never of importance.

No matter what senses are involved, hunting must go on, especially as summer lengthens and the cubs demand more and more to eat. From their earliest childhood—from the time when their eyes either have not or have just opened—the offspring come to regard their parents' mouths as food dispensers. Naturally, when hungry, they want to look into these dispensers in the hope of finding something good. This gives rise to a strange habit. Wishing to calm their little ones' constant demands, parent foxes open their mouths, even when empty, to let the cubs have a look. This may have a slight effect, but ritual tricks of this kind cannot fill the belly. And the parents are forced to forget their fatigue and continue the search, which becomes harder and harder as the grasses of the fields grow deeper. At times such as these, food taken from the habitations of man and fish carcasses picked up on the seashore appear with increased regularity in the den.

This brings me to the problem of chicken thievery. The feud

between the local poultry breeders and the foxes is of long standing. A sympathetic friend, once the chairman of the poultry-breeders' union in our town, obliged me by observing for six months a family of foxes living near his farm. In payment, one night the fox family stole twenty-four of his fowl. What could I say? My friend was unlikely to be consoled by the reminder that research demands sacrifices. (The fox family survived through that winter.)

As I have said, foxes living near the seashore bring home fish when hunting conditions in the grass fields become difficult. One vixen I observed dragged in not only the dead fish that washed up on the beach, but also a large trout that had obviously been caught by a human. Where could she have gotten it? Out of curiosity, I visited a fisherman's watch shack within the range of activity of that particular vixen and learned that in one night a fox had hauled away the contents of two boxes filled with fish—including trout. Each box contained about eight kilograms of fish. Probably she had dragged them out, buried them, and then taken them home one by one as the need arose. The guard in the shack glowered at me and announced that this theft had caused considerable financial loss. I hung my head. But I could not find it in my heart to blame the vixen, who, weary with hunting, had dragged heavy burdens of food to her cubs. Besides, she was molting and already beginning to look more than a little tired and wretched.

SUMMER In July the flowers of the fields vie with each other in loveliness. The summer birds are busily raising the singers of the next season in the breakwind groves, where sometimes the bright gold of the yellow flycatcher flashes through the shadows.

The heat even gets the best of the hard-working parent foxes. They pant as they hunt now and rest in the shade in the middle of the day. Except in time of absolute necessity, the cubs stay under bushes and in the grass without going into the den. Most activity is confined to the morning and evening hours.

Weighing about three kilograms each, the cubs have gained enough experience not to horrify me by mistaking wild dogs for their mother. No longer confined to their parents and each other for playmates, they begin to find toys: twigs, shells, legs of dead birds, pig bones, pebbles, and other things that they scramble for, hide from each other, and in general employ to pass the time. Gradually, they come to prefer moving toys. They chase wildly after wind-swaying grasses or feathers. If a breeze stirs up two or three feathers at a time, there is a wild to-the-death battle with first teeth and then forepaws and hind paws. Obviously, cub fun is training for later serious work.

I gave a name to each of the cubs Muni was rearing that year: Musashi, Matahachi, Takuan, Shiwa, and Akemi. Musashi was the frailest of the litter, but Akemi died at the end of June. They began showing interest in moving objects at about the end of July. Like most other fox cubs, they started with the down and feathers from the breasts of birds their parents had killed for food. Takuan was the most ardent admirer of feather play. At about the same time, they began to amuse themselves with the grasses waving in the wind. One morning Takuan chased a butterfly. He did not catch it, but before long he aimed for a fly, and then a grasshopper, which he caught and taste-tested. As if it were contagious, the pursuit of insects soon caught on among all the other cubs. One evening I watched them leaping and running after bugs in the late light of day. No longer playing, they were now hunting in earnest.

Play and sopshistication of hunting techniques were not the only stimulants for bug hunting, nor was it limited to the cubs in Muni's litter. Examinations of the droppings of foxes of various areas showed a high percentage of insect refuse, indicating that, at last, the tireless efforts of the parents were insufficient to the gargantuan appetites of the growing children.

By now the cubs traveled afield from the den, extending their radius of movement almost to the limits of their parents' hunting zones. But they were never gone for long, and it was usually possible to see most of them around the entrance to the den.

One day our research center received reports of foxes in places where none had been spotted before. This meant that cubs were now leaving the dens, traveling considerable distances with their parents, and remaining away for several days. Earlier the parents had distinctly disliked having any of the cubs follow them, and they would scold and chase them back if they tried. Now the parents adopted the reverse attitude. Not only did they permit the cubs to follow, they actively encouraged and invited them. Only one or two of the cubs could accompany the parents at a time. Even when heavy rain fell, they would not return to the den, since taking care of themselves in inclement weather was part of the training they were undergoing.

There was much for the cubs to learn that was absolutely new. They had to see how to hide from men and stray dogs. They had to observe the correct way to catch a field mouse, and how to locate places where it is safe to rest. They had to learn how to store up on sleep and food, how to brave mooing cows, and how to get out of the way of the roaring, two-eyed automobile monsters if they were trapped by them in the middle of a road. Not all the young escaped the wheels of these predators: we received many reports of foxes killed by cars. Aside from the period immediately after birth, this training phase is the most dangerous and deadly in a fox's life. Many of the cubs who set out on a trip with their parents never saw their dens again.

If the way was perilous for the ones traveling with the parents, insecurity was the lot of those left in the den. They lacked food, and there was nothing to protect them from stray dogs or to ensure that their parents would return.

At about this stage in the family development, territorial limits, heretofore strictly observed, lose their meaning. Since the male fox's duty is more to protect the family from intrusion, when the territory ceases to have significance, so does he, at which point he is likely to disappear. First, he will be gone for two days, then five, until finally he virtually evaporates. When this happens, the value of the den and its surroundings as a place of safety is lost. All of this is one more milestone on the road to independence for the young.

FALL By August the grass has grown as tall as it will, the Sea of Okhotsk begins to heave and swell, and migratory birds store as much food as possible, preparing to leave Hokkaido. The nights grow cold, and the foxes, whose family life was almost entirely disrupted by training trips in July, begin to assemble again. For me, observations were uninteresting as long as they were away. Now a serious change is about to occur in their way of life.

As they all return to the den, the cubs begin to play again. But they no longer use sticks or twigs, and playing among themselves is no longer as simple as it was. Their skills at attack have become refined and sharpened. Since they all know the lay of the land around the den, there is no place for them to hide from each other. For some time, display ceremonies indicating hierarchy have existed among the cubs. They use the so-called defeated posture and the protective-threat posture. In the former, the individual pins its ears back, tucks its tail between its legs, and rolls on its back in front of the individual to whom it is indicating submission. The protective threat is similar, except that the defeated individual barks sharply and wrinkles its nose. Ordinarily, when one cub adopts this posture, whatever quarrel has been under way is considered to have ended. But in the late phase of family life, submission poses cease to have effect, and play takes on an element of desperation and tragedy.

Before long, the mother fox begins to squabble with and bite her offspring. For instance, the family of a vixen I named Bacchus—four cubs: Gin, White Horse, Johnny Walker Black, and Johnny Walker Red—was about to experience the dispersal ritual. Four days after they were reunited in their den with the end the training journeys, biting bouts gradually started. On the morning of August 5, Bacchus attacked. Before long Gin, the best developed male of the litter, had disappeared from the family circle. Next Bacchus attacked Johnny Walker Black, another well-developed cub about equal to his mother in weight. Bacchus forced him out of the deep grass where he had been hiding and began to bite him. Johnny Walker Black put up a fight, but there was no doubt about who would win. No trace of maternity was left in Bacchus when she drove her cub across the meadow. The bonds between Gin and Johnny Walker Black and their mother had been broken. They were no longer her cubs, but were, rather, enemies to be kept out of her territory. Only two days passed between Gin's disappearance and that of Johnny Walker Red.

The same kind of ceremonial punishment to drive the young from the lair or nest is observable in other animals and in birds. In these cases, as in that of foxes, it means that the young are full grown and must now act independently. The parents vanish, and the new adults must go their ways alone.

The end of August, and a few late-blooming field poppies are tossed in the autumn winds sweeping over the meadows. I have practically no chance to meet foxes any more. The cubs have dispersed and, after the harsh experience of the biting ritual, are highly wary. The parents almost never return to the dens, though they sometimes capriciously leave a few tracks in the vicinity.

With the break-up of the families, the territories so jealously guarded from the time of the cold winter lose all meaning. The foxes have set out on journeys to find new places to live. Still, I go out in the hope that maybe one or two animals are left for me to observe. All things are now secrets in the tall, withered grass. I have lived with foxes for such a long time that the autumn is a sad time for me. Until the first snows powder the fields, I wander about discouraged. At these times, I always remember the vixen I named Tōhachi.

She was my first. She introduced me to the fox world, the exciting, bewitching realm where I saw things that often struck cords of response deep inside me.

Foolishly forgetting the difference between the world of wild animals and that of human beings, I did what I could to help Tōhachi in her desperate struggle to feed her young. I brought her food. She soon responded generously and would come considerable distances to meet my car. She permitted me to make fairly detailed examinations of her way of life. I shared my lunches with her—she was displeased unless we split even the smallest things half and half. Most of my early tests on the psychology of foxes were performed on Tōhachi. I was as enthralled by her and her children as if I actually wore King Solomon's ring and could understand what they said.

It was when the cold wind was blowing and the first snow whitened the ground under the dead grasses that she and her whole litter were destroyed by a devil's meat bomb.

A devil's meat bomb is a simple, hideously effective hunting weapon. An explosive and a detonating agent are mixed and put in some strong-smelling meat. An animal takes one bite, and its brain and lower jaw are blasted away.

In the summer days of my entrancement, she had come to trust me. And knowledge of the naiveté and helplessness with which she must have taken this piece of deadly meat intensified my suffering immensely. By not teaching her to know human selfishness, and ugliness, and with my affection and in my self-satisfaction with our relationship, I had hastened her death.

Tōhachi was not only my friend, but also my mentor, for she taught me the danger of allowing human emotions to enter into my relationships with animals. I learned much from her. In the years since then, many other foxes have become my friends and teachers, but I have never again tried to break down the barrier between their world and mine. Tōhachi's legacy to me was the awareness of the need to maintain emotional distance in relations with creatures of the forests and meadows. My close friendship with her ended in sorrow, suffering, and increased maturity.

EPILOGUE The Sea of Okhotsk once again rages against the blue-black dunes, and the north winds hold meadows, forests, and plains in icy chains. The ground where the fox cubs played has hardened for the long winter sleep. As I stand at the mouth of the Ponyanbetsu, these glacial fields have a different meaning: they are both the site of the investigations I have made and the field where I hope to make new ones. Once a kaleidoscope of many colors changing from spring to summer and into fall, the meadows and plains are now monochrome white. Only a few fox tracks mark those places that but weeks ago were still vibrant with activity. Land that has reared countless cubs in the past and will rear countless more in the future is magically secretive.

At midnight the roaring of the sea drops to stillness. The temperature plummets, and people speak of first ice floes. That evening I had seen—from far across the snow fields—a fox retreating into the distance. It looked like Tōhachi.

Four Seasons of Family Life: Photographs

Winter

Under endless stretches of ice floes, the Sea of Okhotsk silently waits for spring. Grasses bend under heavy snowy burdens. Soundless are the unbroken lines of hills, until the blizzards howl and the creaking-dry snow swirls. After the storm, stillness. Nothing moves. Then across the snow on the dunes a single line of tracks suggests life. The line passes hillocks and meadows, only to disappear into a grove beyond a small river. The tracks are the footprints of a vixen who has walked, without eating, for ten days. A flame of life deep within her is searching. It is the season of vulpine romance.

Spring

Strong southern winds crack the ice floes and drive them groaning away, and the Sea of Okhotsk recalls how to speak with the returning waterfowl. The restless Ezo red frogs sing in chorus in the bright streams of melted snow. Sounds ride on the wings of the swans gliding back to the lake. Sweetbrier sends young shoots over the sandy dunes just above a dark den where new cubs cry for the first time.

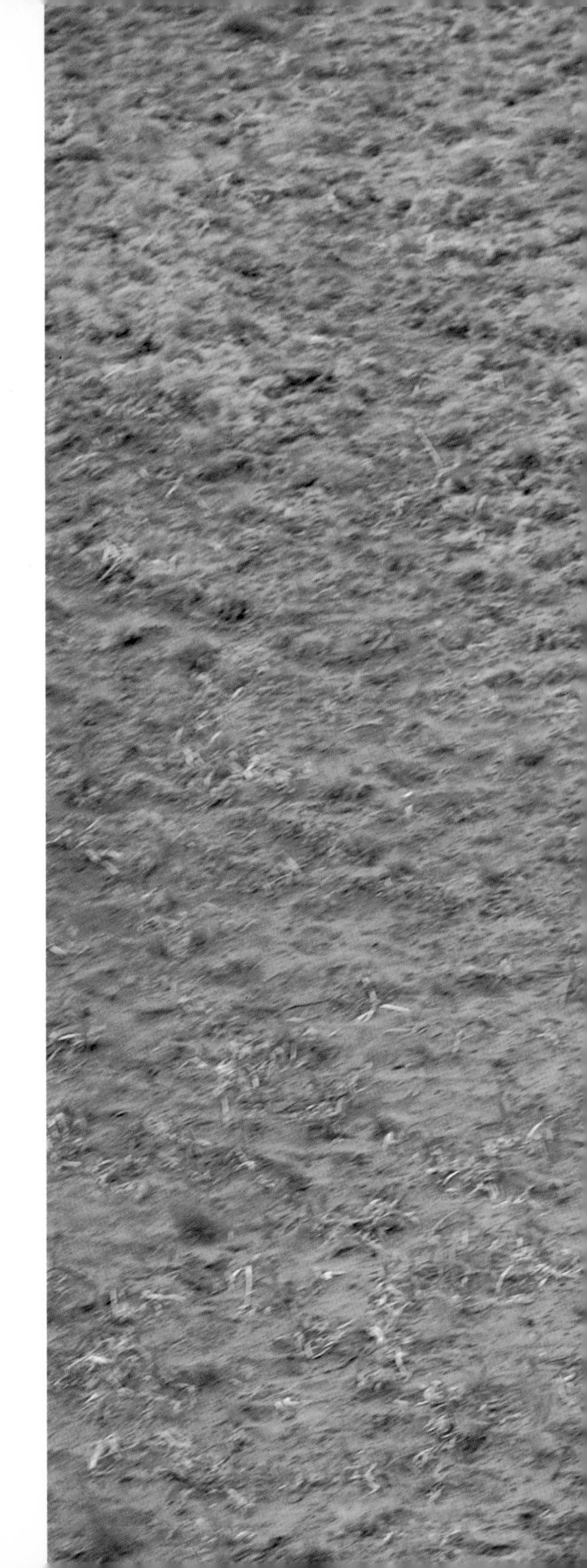

Summer

The Sea of Okhotsk is at its summer bluest. The waving green grasses of the dunes and fields, glimmering with yellow wild clover, orange field lilies, purple wild irises, and red sweetbrier, shelter small creatures, such as summer birds busily raising their young. The loud barking of the cubs proclaims their eagerness to be off on their first training trips.

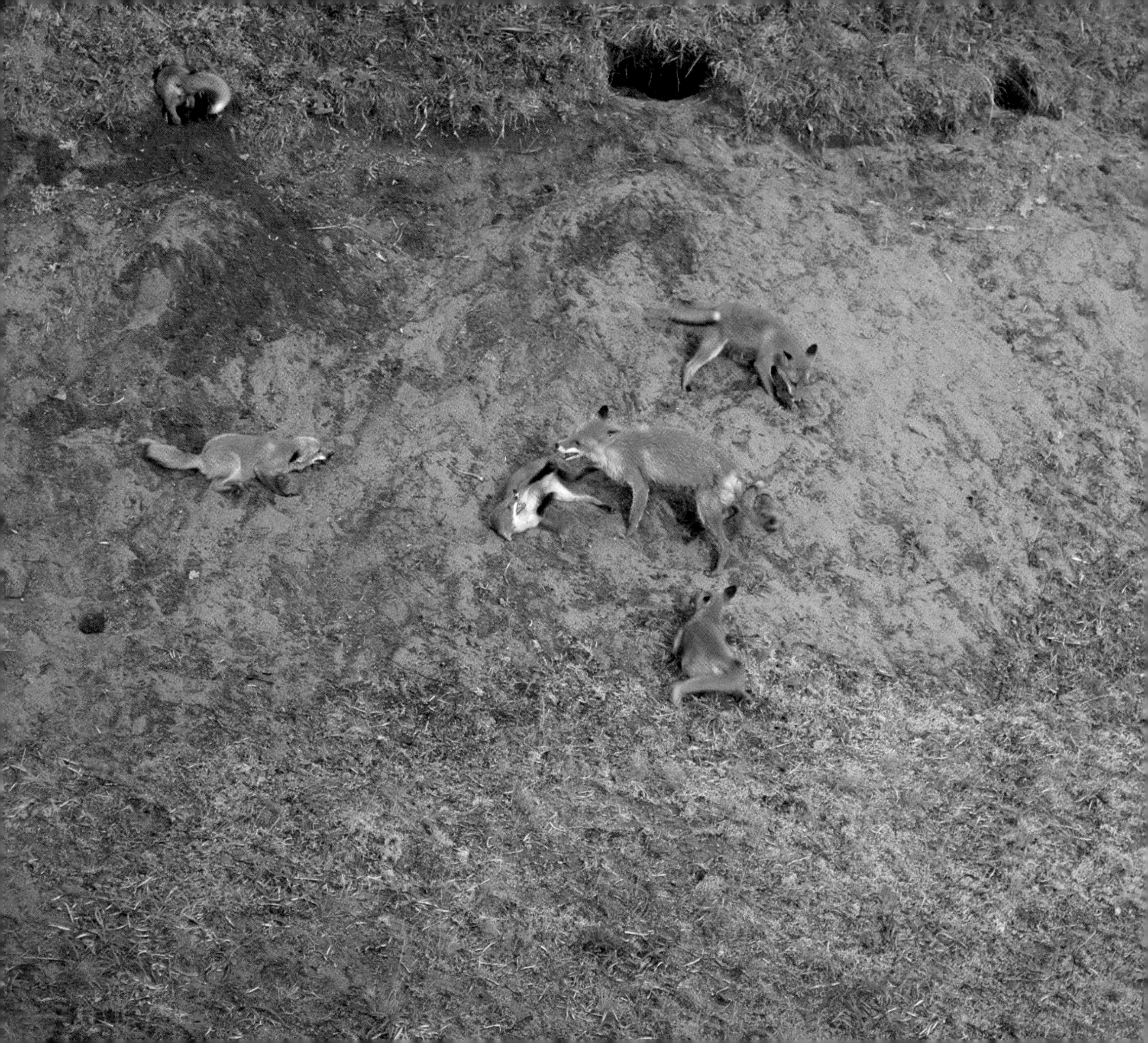

Fall

The blue-black Sea of Okhotsk thunders white-capped toward the dunes. Late-blooming pink field poppies cast furtive shadows on the fields. Birds from beach and field have flown away. The Shiretoko Mountains are clothed in autumn, as the vixen chasing her young away from the den stirs a tumult of shadow in the dying grass. Sad, lonely cries float on the wind as the fox family is sundered and the young go their ways alone.

Commentaries on the Photographs

WINTER

This was my first good look at the foxes this severe winter. Vulpine love affairs last only thirty-six hours. This is all the time the foxes are permitted for romance in the long year.

No hardship or danger is taken into consideration in the pursuit of love. Like the characters in some of the famous plays of the Japanese dramatist Chikamatsu Monzaemon, one who thinks of insignificant things like peril is disqualified as a lover.

The vixen stops from time to time to urinate. The male following her does likewise. This pattern of actions, which is carried out through the whole day, seems to communicate the feelings of one member of the pair to the other.

For a few days before and after mating, the pair sleep quite close together, though under ordinary circumstances they slumber apart in whatever place appeals to each. It looked to me as if they enjoyed the dusty snow whirled up from time to time by the wind.

The male's occasional bark may be intended to apprise any rivals in the neighborhood of his presence. Or maybe it is a love serenade for the vixen walking ahead.

The romance begins when the ice floes are forming on the Sea of Okhotsk. I have seen tracks leading from far away across the ice, as if the foxes' true homes were somewhere way out there.

When mating starts, the foxes stop eating. In the frozen winter wastes, they lose all appetite for food.

On mating day, he acts in a violent fashion, and she runs away. If he catches up with her, she turns on him with mouth open and teeth bared in what looks more like a fight than a romance. This kind of behavior sometimes goes on for over six hours.

Occasionally she chases him. Chase and flee, flee and chase. On these days their tracks in the snow are a jumble.

When the love play is drawing to a close, the two animals stand on their hind legs with front paws on each other's backs. They hold this pose for a few seconds, as if to reaffirm their feelings.

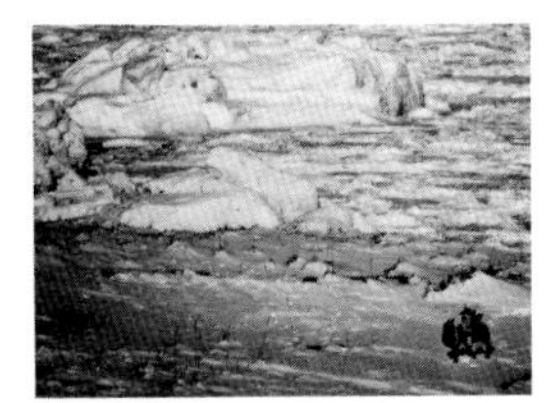

Mating completed, the vixen is once again often alone as the male travels far and wide to the limits of his territory. Nonetheless, they generally meet once a day.

The time is too cold, too sad. Why did the gods decide to make this the foxes' season of love? Still, there is something wonderful about romance on the brink of the ice floes.

About one week after mating, the vixen's appetite picks up, and she becomes a hunter of great terror for the Ezo field hare. Often her hunt is a failure. But the hare will have seen his last day if the snow is a little too deep or if he is in less than top fettle.

Since the snow has hidden most of the foxes' usual prey, the rare catch is a treasure not to be wasted. What remains after one meal is hidden in the snow—a natural deep freeze. One Ezo snow hare will feed a fox for about ten days.

Under the snow covering the fields, small creatures bustle. In the earnest hunt for food to nourish the cubs in her womb, the vixen may leap to an attack after hearing the sounds of mouse feet under the white cover.

On one rare occasion when this vixen was full, she came upon a mouse, and instead of eating it, she observed its motions and did no more than play with it for a few minutes.

When the warm sun hints at coming spring, the male, who had been guarding the periphery of the territory, starts coming closer to the mouth of the den. The vixen's movements are becoming sluggish, and her tracks in the snow are irregular.

He seems to know about the cubs inside the vixen's womb. Sometimes he takes her hunting with him and either gives her his catches or buries them hurriedly under the snow.

In the farmland beyond the dunes I saw a single fox barking as it walked. As springtime approaches, loners like this one want families of their own.

I have seen unfamiliar females at the edge of the windbreak forest. Pregnant vixens assiduously avoid encounters with them at this phase. Undesired meetings can cause miscarriages.

A male and a vixen hunting on the frozen surface of the lake. Only in winter can they catch prey on the small island in the middle of the lake; in other seasons it is inaccessible, and they must hunt on the far shore.

When the typical strong south winds of this area begin to blow, the ice floes of the Sea of Okhotsk move northward. Two Hokkaido foxes, sleek and seeming to enjoy the arrival of spring, cross one of the remaining blocks of winter ice.

As if memories of their romance lingered with the ice of the sea, the two of them visit each of the remaining masses of the floe and then disappear. She is surprisingly slender to be pregnant, and her teats are only slightly visible.

SPRING

Hurrying homeward along the thaw ponds in the fields, where red Ezo frogs vie with each other in singing their short spring choruses.

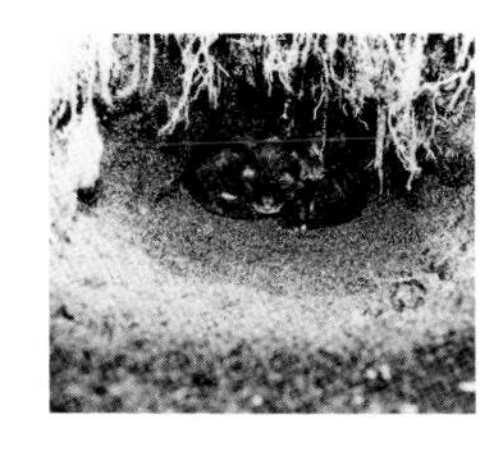

The cubs cry softly in the dark, sandy room at the innermost end of the den, which is dug in the southern slope of a hill in the grassy plains. On the fourteenth postnatal day, their eyes open. The time is drawing near for them to be able to go out of their home.

Dazzling and warm, the cub's first sunlight. They are in the womb for fifty-two days and remain with the mother in the dark of the den for another twenty-four. The cloudy little eyes are too weak to distinguish the parents, even at close range.

The parents are responsible for the hunt and for the safety of the den zone. The cubs are left alone much of the time, and they look forward impatiently to the time when the father brings home food.

As long as the cubs were very small and remained in the den, the vixen nursed them lying down. But as soon as they are able to come outside, she stands for the nursing operation. Breast feeding, the cubs' happiest moments, occurs about five times daily.

Spring weather is usually fair in this part of Hokkaido. Formerly the cubs never left the den without mother. But enticed by bright skies and high clouds, they begin to venture forth—not more than about fifty centimeters, it is true—on their own.

Playing with their parents and relishing the varied menu made possible by hunting trips are the cubs' joys. When the male repairs the mouth of the den, only his tail is visible (upper right).

No longer satisfied with the immediate vicinity of the den, the cubs begin to move farther afield in their play. But mother brings them back if they go too far.

Then they follow their father to the top of the dune behind the den. But their eyes, limited to a range of about twenty-five meters, cannot see the hills in the distance, the houses of human beings, and the mountains still farther away.

One morning they quietly trailed along behind mother, and they found out for the first time that the sea was close at hand. With a sharp bark, mother scolded them and sent them scurrying back the way they had come. They never knew that people were fishing in the distance.

The cubs steadily grow bigger and, no matter how much they eat, hungrier. They remember those days in the dark lair when food came from mother's mouth and are always eager to take a look inside her oral cavity to see if maybe there is still something edible in there.

When the summer birds return, both parents are away hunting most of the time. The cubs are lonely at being left in the den.

The vixen's hunting range has extended to the farmlands and the ponds beyond. As I watch her go out, I wonder—probably together with the cubs—what she will bring home for supper in the evening.

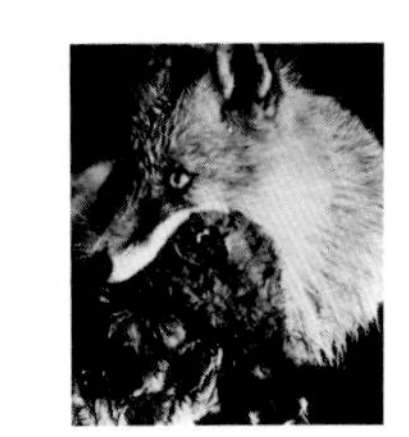

One morning, the father came back with a large Ezo hare. Though his coat was shabby because of molting and his tail looked like a wornout broom, the fox's bright eyes were keen and sharp.

When spring finally comes, the cubs romp and chase butterflies through dandelion fields.

Enticed by the dandelion world that stretches far into the distance, a cub suddenly finds himself alone and cries until he hears mother's reassuring footsteps.

SUMMER

As the green of the fields deepens, the cubs come to look more like foxes. Their eyes now have a golden gleam, and though they are still frail-looking, they have the russet color and the sleek look of adults.

Frightened but curious, the cubs warily approach a snake that the parents have brought home. Then suddenly the snake rears up.

The snake looked worn out and weak, but its tail was still moving. When it tried to hurl itself free, the fox, with hair bristling on its back, killed it.

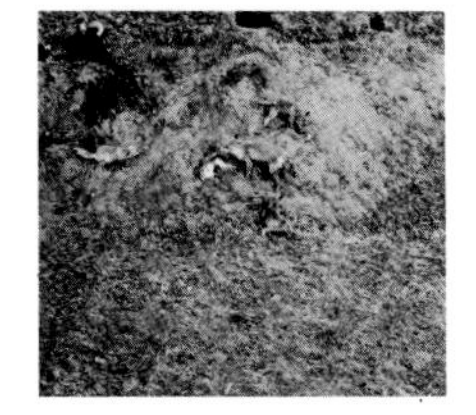

The cubs' bellies ceaselessly demand filling, and the long hunting trips combined with molting make the parents very unsightly. Nonetheless, the very demands that their offspring make seem to be a source of happiness.

In July, though still a little confused by the strange world, the cubs begin to follow their parents on slightly longer jaunts. The parents do not seem to object too much.

One morning the mother takes the cubs with her on a trip. She makes a clucking sound to urge them forward if they try to turn back. They seem to be headed for the open meadows beyond the pasture.

A slight waving in the grass, and a cub leaps upward into the air. Perhaps it was a frog. But this is their first trip, and any unusual motion sends the cubs leaping.

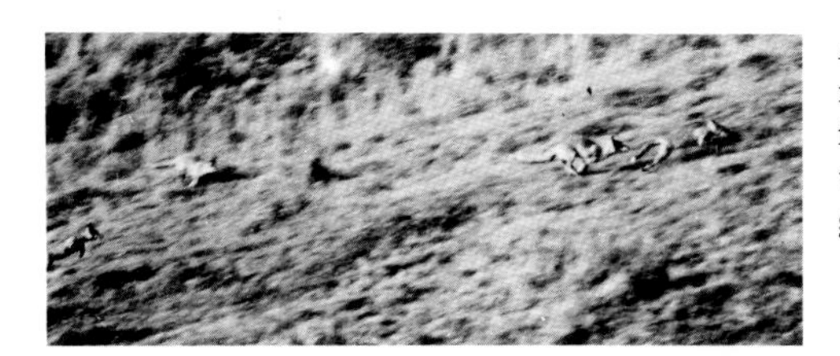

A strange animal smell is strong in the meadow. The anxious cubs hesitate for a minute. But then the temptation to sprint through this unobstructed grassland is too great.

The owner of the strange animal smell. At first the cubs seemed to think of running away, but curiosity gets the best of them. The strange creature's snorting breath is a shock.

Immediately after crossing two long rails stretching out in both directions, they are terrified by the tremendous sound of a huge, clanking thing that comes racing along those iron tracks. The mother has a hard time gathering the dispersed cubs. For the first time they sleep away from the den.

The morning after the first night out—they slept in a thicket of sweetbrier. If they think of the cubs left at home at all, the idea is soon driven from their minds by the sunlight gleaming on the dew and the desire to dash through the grass.

Dripping wet with dew, they run across a world of meadow that seems to reach to the clouds. Before any of them is aware of it, they are racing again.

After the race, the journey continues across the hill and through a grove. Then, in a small pasture, another creature with a strong smell. This one has a long tail that suddenly swishes from side to side.

As the training trip ends, they come upon a house for the first time in their lives. No one lives in this one, but it has a familiar smell: other foxes must have made this place their home. Perhaps as the former fox residents did, the mother climbs to the roof for a look at the surroundings.

Back at home in the grass fields near the den—with the mountains of Shiretoko in the distance—they feel at ease. The cubs who stayed home this time must make a journey soon—before the autumn winds begin to blow.

After a number of training trips have been made, they all live around the den for a while longer. Though almost fully grown and difficult to distinguish from the parents, the cubs still never miss a chance to try to get a little extra attention from father or mother.

Fights among the cubs are no longer childish play. In earlier months the cub who lost in a game rolled over and exposed his belly—his most vulnerable part—to the winner. No longer. Now when the fight seems to be over, one chases the other all the way across the field.

At the end of July the cubs stop playing among themselves or with their parents, choosing rather to keep themselves entertained alone. They hide pebbles in the grass or bury bird wings. When they get bored, they may take a wing in their mouths and jump upward with it.

Soon they begin chasing—and catching and eating—grasshoppers and butterflies. At twilight, this cub is leaping in pursuit of an insect.

What began as play becomes serious hunting. By the end of July, cub droppings are made up almost entirely of the hard wings of insects. In this case, a quail may have been the cubs' first large prey.

The kinds of animals they catch change. Fledgling birds predominate, and sometimes the cubs chase field mice.

Windless days are the best for hunting. If they listen carefully, the cubs can hear the footsteps of small animals at the bases of the wild poppies. As soon as they hear a sound, they leap up and pounce on the clump of grass from which the sound came.

Nothing this time. The cubs have learned to hold the same position for a few minutes and to leap lightly and softly. Who taught them? No one.

Often the parents do not come home. The cubs have learned to protect themselves from danger, and the territory—so jealously guarded during the cold winter—is less significant. The father seems to have lost interest in his duties. Not coming home again tonight!

FALL

Suddenly everything is different. The mother begins to menace the cubs, who let out barks that sound like screams. It seems to be only a minor matter, but it is actually the beginning of worse.

At first confused, the cubs soon learn that mother is serious when she bites them wildly and threatens them. Before long, they run away from her. The males go first. The females run away, but come back time and time again. With each of the mother's hysterical biting attacks, the number of cubs in the brood diminishes. This ritual is proof that they are all now able to fend for themselves.

The mother brings food back to the now empty nest and calls. One female cub appears, and the mother instantaneously chases her away. The daughter is now only an unwanted intruder.

Fall has arrived. At twilight, a lone fox sits on the railway tracks. He hunts in this area and is probably waiting for a train and the leftovers the travelers throw out the window. He looks sad.

No longer a cub, this full-grown lone male hunts leftover corn in a field. The woods are full of mice, but foxes seem to like corn and sweet berries.

As the lake begins to freeze, a fox who looks like one of the cubs I have been observing watches the swans that have just returned from Siberia. He sits there until the sudden flight of one of the birds sends him scurrying.

The fallen leaves tell where the field mice are. With nose in the leaves, the fox travels for some meters. After having found the entrance to a lair where striped squirrels hibernate, he works for forty minutes, trying to dig the creatures out, and then gives up.

For a while the fox tries to ignore the distinctive warning sound of the Ezo squirrel pounding on the tree trunk with its paws. But curiosity will not let him rest until he moves around the tree where the squirrel sits and stands on his hind legs for a better view.

Then he makes up his mind to climb. Though he is clumsy, he makes it to a height of about four meters. He merely falls to descend.

Winter on the Sea of Okhotsk. The always-busy sandpipers have flown south. In winter fur, one fox appears daily on the beach in search of dead fish or bird carcasses that wash up.

Sweetbrier, greatly appreciated by the foxes for its sweet-sour taste, gradually disappears, and it is time for snow. The long, white world is drawing near.

The drizzle of this evening is tomorrow's snow, in which I will begin once again to decipher the story that is written in fox tracks: last night's sleeping place, only two field mice here, and so on.

Snow at the roots of the dead grass. The sound of rifles. The cruelest season for the foxes, and all I can do is scream to them to run! run!

Fecund fields that bred the cubs of this season and that will breed next season's silently guard their secrets beneath the snow. How many foxes will make love on this ice floe this year?

Facts About Foxes

The ubiquity of the fox in folklore throughout the world testifies to the persistent relations between this animal and mankind and to the chances they have always had of encountering one another. Interestingly enough, however, the fox has never been truly tamed, as dogs have. And a great deal of misinformation is widespread about the fox's way of life. The following pages are an attempt to rectify this situation by providing some general vulpine biology.

Classification and Distribution Members of the dog family, to which the foxes belong, are widely distributed from Africa to Eurasia and North and South America. Among them, the foxes, of which there are ten recognized species, are among the most numerous and flourishing. These are distributed practically everywhere that dogs occur, with the exception of South America, and they vary according to the region in which they live. Most of them, however, occupy fairly limited zones and have evolved in conformity with their environments. Of all the foxes, the red fox has the widest distribution and has most stubbornly protected its identity and unity. Fossils of the red fox are found as early as the middle Pleistocene epoch, and the type seems to have branched, as did the Arctic fox and the Kossack fox, from ancestors that lived in the early Pleistocene. In general, the red fox lives in the temperate zones of North America and Eurasia. The Japanese fox, a local variety of the red fox, is of two types: the smaller *Hondo-kitsune*, distributed throughout the islands of Honshu, Shikoku, and Kyushu; and the somewhat larger *Kita-kitsune*, or Hokkaido fox, of Hokkaido and Sakhalin. Variation in size, in accordance with the Bergman rule that northern mammalian species are larger than southern ones, is observable in these animals as well. On the average, the northern or Hokkaido fox is between sixty and eighty centimeters long in the body and has a tail of from thirty-seven to forty-four centimeters. The male is larger than the female. The back is reddish brown, and the hair on the lips, chest, belly, and tip of the tail is white. There is some black hair on the front sides of the forepaws. Tail color may vary considerably. Sometimes the back is more golden than red-brown, and some individuals have dark, cross-shaped markings on the back.

Habitat The habitat adaptability of the fox is astounding. They are known to live at all altitudes, ranging from the seashore to the timberline. But, although they now live in the vicinities of fishing and farming villages, in grassy meadows, and in scrub thickets, it is likely that they prefer scrubby undergrowth at the border between forests and meadows. For instance, on Mount Dazetsu in Hokkaido, foxes are plentiful in low farmlands, on the edges of replanted forests, and in the highland meadows above the great forests, but are scarce in the forest itself. When human beings clear forests for the purpose of small-scale agriculture, they create mixed environments that are ideal for foxes. And this has the effect of bringing foxes and men closer together in a way that is reflected in folklore.

Large-scale, standardized agriculture, on the other hand, sharply curtails the amount of land on which the fox can live. In the parts of Japan where land has been extensively converted into wet-rice fields, the fox has virtually disappeared. Still, in some areas, especially in Hokkaido, where dry-field farming is important and where windbreak and other small forests have either been preserved or reforested, foxes find places that satisfy their minimal requirements. Furthermore, the proximity of dairy and poultry farms on Hokkaido makes food provision easier. In such areas and around some Japanese cities, the numbers of foxes are slowly increasing.

Dens Within its home range, the fox usually has one or two large dens where offspring are born and raised, and other smaller ones to be used as emergency refuges. The nature of the hole in which the den is made depends on terrain and other factors. The fox uses natural crevices and caves in the rocky surface of the ground, or digs holes for itself. Sometimes foxes live under the floorboards of abandoned houses or huts near farming villages or in ditches that are no longer used. Interesting stories are told of foxes cooperating with other animals. In Europe, foxes are said to expand and remodel for family use holes left by the burrowing hare. They are even said to share dens with badgers and wildcats. Even stranger, they sometimes live in the same lairs with hares, marmots, and owls—creatures on which the fox usually feeds—and do no harm to their coinhabitants.

Recent investigations in Hokkaido and Kyushu have shown that foxes dig dens more often on slopes than on flat land. In Hokkaido, they often use holes left when trees are uprooted to clear pasturage. Though they will dig dens in ground with a variety of coverages, ranging from deciduous, broad-leaved trees to such trees as larch, and in sandy dunes, they avoid dank, gloomy, evergreen forest zones. Even should they live in a forest, they are never far from its edge.

Den compositions vary according to locale. Research on four fox lairs in Kyushu showed that each had from three to nine entrances. From each entrance, the tunnel turned sharply downward for from fifty to one hundred centimeters and then leveled out to lead four or five meters inward. All of the tunnels were interconnected. Each of the two lairs excavated in Hokkaido had two entrances and horizontal holes connected at the innermost ends. The tunnels penetrated inward for from six to ten meters.

As long as conditions remain favorable, foxes use the same den every year, expanding and increasing the number of entrances as time goes by. Though there may be as few as one and as many as thirteen entrances, the average number is four. The interconnected tunnels are from twenty to twenty-five centimeters wide and about twenty centimeters high. This means that the parent foxes must crawl through them. In the dens of Hokkaido foxes, there are along the tunnels small (from forty to sixty centimeters in diameter) round chambers just big enough for the parent fox to curl up and sleep. In the cases of the Hokkaido foxes, usually nothing is spread on the den floor, though hair from the belly of the vixen is found in the chambers where young are reared. In Kyushu, leaves and grasses are sometimes found in the nursery chambers of dens. Frequently the droppings of the offspring and the remains of carcasses of prey are found scattered in the chambers and tunnels. Investigations have shown that, at times other than August and September, the dens are put to a different use. It is said that fox dens open southward, but examination of about one hundred in Japan has shown no clear directional orientation.

BREEDING Ordinarily foxes breed once yearly. Males track down vixens in heat by the odor of the females' urine. A number of males may congregate and fight for the favors of one vixen, and one vixen does not necessarily limit herself to one male: she may copulate with several in succession. Mating season varies with locale: in southern regions, it takes place from the end of December into January; in northern regions, from early February until early April. In Hokkaido, mating reaches a peak in the period from the end of January to the middle of February, when pairs or single females followed by several males are frequently to be seen. The period of heat is divided into an anterior phase, lasting about thirteen days, and a phase of optimum readiness, lasting two or three days. At this time, the female will become impregnated. She will give birth, after a period of fifty-one to fifty-three days, to from three to eight (average three to five) cubs. In Hokkaido, birth usually takes place during the period between late March and late April. Though at birth cubs of both sexes are about equal in number, by the time they reach maturity, fatality will usually have altered the ratio to from 1.2 to 2 males to 1 female.

As a rule one male and one female rear the brood, although sometimes two females with offspring cooperate under the surveillance of a single male. And occasionally males and females with no young of their own are included in the group.

For about three weeks after copulation, the male brings food to the vixen. For several weeks following birth, the vixens leaves the den only for water and evacuation, and the male is responsible for providing all food. When the cubs can finally go out of the den, the male brings them food as well, though it is usually first given to the vixen, who then passes it to the young. During the period in which the young must be protected, the male and the female are often seen in the undergrowth or on a rising near the mouth of the den, where they are on the lookout for danger. When a prospective enemy draws close, they bark or otherwise indicate peril and send the young scurrying back into the lair. For the first three weeks or so, the mother lies on her side in the nest to nurse her cubs. When they can go out of the lair, however, she nurses them in a standing position.

Growth of the Cubs Weighing from fifty to one-hundred-and-fifty grams at birth, the cubs, whose eyes open on the fourteenth day, begin to take solid food on the twentieth day. By the time they leave the lair, four months after birth, they weigh about three kilograms. In the autumn, six months after birth, they look like fully grown adults, though they are still somewhat light and will not reach the lower limits of the average weight for the red fox until the first period of heat in the winter.

At birth, cub fur is dark grayish brown. About a month after birth, long, light brown hair begins to appear. By the time they leave the den, they will have a coat very much like the parents' summer fur. Longer, denser hair will come in with the onset of autumn. After they have developed a full coat, they will shed once yearly in the spring-summer period. They learn to distinguish the form and actions of the parents and how to tell foxes from other animals during the period between the twenty-fourth and thirty-sixth postnatal days. Four months after birth, the parents either ignore them or become positively hostile, and the young adults leave the lair and disperse.

Dispersal According to a report for the period between April and June of a given year, 926 foxes were tagged and released in Illinois and Ohio in the United States. The information obtained from this test showed that at the end of September, young foxes born the previous spring were still living in the vicinity of the places where they were born. But dispersal began in the early part of October. It started first with the males; by the middle of October, eight males had gone 23.7 kilometers from their birthplaces, whereas six females in the same period had gone only 3.2 kilometers. The difference in dispersal time seems related to sexual maturity. The males mature in late November or December, but the females do not reach this stage until January or February. Telemetry performed in connection with this same experiment showed that in five days in November one male traveled an average of eleven miles daily. In other words, the animal could cover the whole of its home range in one autumn evening. It is scarcely surprising, then, that one of the foxes recovered was seen to have traveled about one hundred miles in forty-five days. At the rate of eleven miles a day, he could easily have moved the same distance in a month. Males recovered were seen to have moved from 0 to 161.9 (average of 29.4) kilometers from their birthplaces, whereas females moved only from 0 to 83.4 (average of 9.9) kilometers. A total of 82 percent of the females studied were found within 16 kilometers of their birthplaces. In the second year, the animals moved farther afield;

but even so, the males went a greater distance than did the females. Adults and one-year-old cubs alike traveled about in the autumn and winter. Other American experiments have shown that some foxes moved as much as 193 kilometers in 2 years or as much as 392 kilometers in 9 months. In the initial year, 70 percent of one-year-old males moved 8 kilometers from the birthplaces and 90 percent have moved that far by the second year. The percentages are lower for females: 30 percent in the first year and 50 percent in the second. Nonetheless, this high rate of dispersal, which seriously affects individual and group movement, is closely related to the spread of disease and makes it difficult to control population in any given region.

TERRITORY Certain conditions have to be satisfied for a home territory. It must provide a place of rest and refuge. It must offer opportunities for the preparation of dens, the collection of food, and the procurement of water. In addition, it must have some high spots—tree stumps, risings, slopes, and so on—where foxes can rest and sleep, even if snow is on the ground, as long as the day is sunny.

Like dogs, foxes use excrement and urine to mark the boundaries of their territorres. They leave droppings that have a distinctive odor (the result of an anal-glandular secretion) on risings, tree stumps, boulders, and other prominent places to mark off their zones. In addition, they urinate on grass and trees to the same end. Urination of this kind becomes especially frequent in breeding season, and females leave urine and droppings at the mouths of the dens where they intend to rear their young.

Foxes apparently do not guard their entire home territories, some of which have been reported to overlap. Telemetry reports from Minnesota, however, revealed three neighboring home territories that did not overlap and that were apparently used by families living close together as a mechanism to protect independence and guard against aggression. Though the boundaries, which may be natural features like rivers or man-made ones like roads, are not patrolled, they are clearly recognized and avoided by neighboring families. A fox will usually cover all of its own territory once within a period of about two weeks. But the extent of the home territory varies according to climatic conditions and the density of the fox population. Study of tracks in the snow in Michigan revealed that, in the southern part of the state, foxes covered about 3.6 square kilometers a day, whereas, in the north, they covered about 7.3 square kilometers. Similar studies in Hokkaido showed that in farm areas a fox's home territory averages from 2 to 4 square kilometers, but diminishes to from 0.6 to 1 square kilometer when a good supply of food is nearby. In swampy land, on the other hand, the territory sometimes is as large as fifteen square kilometers. Telemetry research performed in one week in the middle of February showed that, in areas of broad-leaved trees, agricultural land, swampy lowland, and land around rivers, home territories of 3 vixens were 5.9, 6.4, and 8.4 square kilometers. Similar research performed in the 6.5 months between February and August showed territories of 2 males to be 3.7 and 4.2 square kilometers.

POPULATION DENSITY AND LIFE SPAN Environmental structure and availability of food largely determine fox-population density. There are usually more foxes per area unit in such favorable places as groves, hilly regions, grassy plains, scrub areas, or sea and lake shores where the fox's natural prey is plentiful. Investigations done in the spring annually for 5 years in European zones where forest and farmland exist in 50–50 ratio showed that there were from 1.46 to 1.04 foxes per square kilometer, with an average value of 0.58 per square kilometer. An investigation made in the land and seashore (about 90 square kilometers) around the town of Koshimizu in the eastern part of Hokkaido in 1970 produced the following results:

forty-one dens were observed, and in twenty-two of them offspring were born, and a total of eighty-five cubs was confirmed. Though, as I have already said, such is not always the case, for the sake of calculation it was assumed that each family consisted of one male, one vixen, and the cubs. This would mean forty-four parents. The total number of foxes for this region in May-June of this year then was 129, or a fairly high population density of 1.4 foxes per square kilometer. In the prebirth winter-spring period there was probably an average of at least 0.5 foxes per square kilometer. Since the number of dens in the zone has not increased much, the population has probably reached a state of saturation. The frequent occurrence of two vixens caring for a brood of cubs may be the outcome of overly dense population.

Because each year a number of foxes equal to the new births either disperses widely or dies, no marked increase in population in the study area occurs yearly, in spite of a high birth rate. Many of the animals who leave the area probably travel to the vicinities of the poultry, pig, and dairy farms that are increasing in both number and scale. Nonetheless, this cannot account for all of the newborn cubs, and the mortality rate must be high among the young. Surveys have shown that only one-sixth of the animals who survive their first winter live to see their second. This indicates a mortality rate of 84 percent. Between the second and third years, about 55 percent die; between the third and fourth, about 57 percent; and between the fourth and fifth, about 40 percent. Furthermore, since the death rate is extremely high in the few months between birth and the first winter, the mortality rate for young foxes is made still higher.

NATURAL ENEMIES AND CAUSES OF DEATH Little detailed information is available on the causes of death among foxes. Young cubs who have just left the den are frequently killed by automobiles, though the percentage of total deaths accounted for by such accidents is unknown. Among natural enemies of the fox are numbered bears, wolves, dogs, wildcats, pumas, leopards, wolverines, hawks and eagles, although how these animals capture and eat foxes is a matter of conjecture. Internal parasites, rabies, and distemper are also said to take their tolls. At one time in Hokkaido, large numbers of foxes died from eating rats and squirrels killed by a powerful poison used for pest control in agricultural areas. But later, when the use of this substance had been outlawed, the fox population recovered.

SENSE PERCEPTION Foxes have well-developed senses of hearing and smell. Their hearing is especially keen. They can detect sounds of frequencies higher than 20,000 cycles, a level imperceptible to human ears. I have observed foxes react to the sound of a leaf falling at a distance of more than ten meters on a windless day. This ability is highly useful in capturing the mice and rats that are staples of the fox diet. The sense of smell gives the fox a general idea of where its prey is located, but for the capture of small animals like mice, more accurate locating is essential. The fox is able to gauge the direction from which a sound is emitted with an accuracy tolerance of only a few degrees. This, plus swift, well-coordinated motion, helps it in the hunt. The fox's upward leap and downward pounce on its prey enable it to capture animals much smaller and more agile than itself. This hunting method is another indication that the fox is most at home in fairly open terrain.

In autumn and winter, the fox must rely largely on berries and dead carcasses for food. Locating the corpses of birds and mice under deep snow requires application of their good sense of smell. I have commented elsewhere (page 14) on the animals' poor eyesight.

ACTIVITY PATTERNS Telemetry research on a limited range in Hokkaido agrees with similar studies performed in the United States and Europe to the effect that foxes have three peaks of daily activity—morning, evening, and the middle of the night—and that they tend to rest in the daytime. But the Hokkaido studies further shows that, at mating time and when there are cubs to feed, foxes are active in the daytime as well. Foxes do not form packs, as do wolves, but prefer rather to operate largely on their own. This partly explains why, though they become fairly accustomed to having human beings around when they are raising cubs, they have never been domesticated. When a number of foxes cohabit in the raising of a litter, hierarchy is established among them and is said to be expressed in ritual actions.

The range of daily movement varies according to the availability of food. In open grass plains in the snow season, a fox may travel as much as twenty-two kilometers daily, though from one to four kilometers daily is common in agricultural land. Studies in Illinois revealed a maximum of 2.4 kilometers a day, whereas trackings in Michigan showed a maximum of 5.8 kilometers a day.

DIET The fox diet is inclusive. Although they rely largely on animal food when it is available, in certain seasons they eat vegetable foods as well. Examinations of the contents of the stomachs of 1,006 foxes taken in the state of Missouri revealed 63 kinds of animal food, 21 kinds of vegetable food, and 2 kinds of food classified as miscellaneous. But of this variety, only 15 kinds of animal food and 1 kind of vegetable food accounted for more than 1 percent of the total. In other words, only a fairly small group of foods was taken in large quantities. The most important foods were rabbits (especially the cottontail, accounting for 36.1 percent), field mice (13.5 percent), and chickens (12.3 percent). Other domesticated animals accounted for 7.7 percent of the total.

Fluctuations in rabbit population over a period of five years were reflected in fluctuations in the number of rabbits eaten. In years when rabbits were scarce, foxes ate more chickens. The percentages remain unaltered in spring, but in summer domestic fowl account for a greater and rabbits and mice a lesser percent. Of course, the locale determines the diet: foxes living where waterfowl are numerous feed on them, those living near animal farms eat the dead bodies or afterbirths of domestic animals, and those living near fishing villages survive on fish. Recent research has shown that in Hokkaido at present more than 40 percent of the fox diet consists of wastes in one way or another related to human beings and their actions.

RELATIONS WITH HUMAN BEINGS In general, the fox is welcomed by farmers for the way it keeps down the rodent population. But since foxes—like other larger predatory animals—tend to increase in numbers more slowly than fecund rodents, sometimes they do not catch up, and harm to crops cannot be prevented. It is therefore necessary to provide good living conditions and ample food for the larger predators in order to control the damaging rodent population. This has been done in Hokkaido, and the rabbit population there is kept at a fairly even level.

But increases in the fox population are now a source of worry, since foxes carry bacteria and parasites that can infect human beings. In the United States and Europe, where great stress is put on controlling rabies, close watch is kept on fox populations. Bounties offered hunters for foxes may be of some help, but this is an expensive method. In some areas—especially in places where epidemics are likely—immunization of foxes, as well as of dogs and cats, is being carried out.

Note on Photography

Although I am not a professional photographer, the long period I took to record fox-family life on film gave me ample time and experience to develop my technique. Altogether I spent twelve years taking the photographs for this study—a period that was far longer than I thought I would need when I first started the project. During that time I took approximately 70,000 shots from which the photographs for this book were chosen.

The only requirement I set for a fox to become a part of the subject matter for this study was that it be living in the area where I was working. Thus there were 120 fox families that came under my observation during these twelve years. But of those, I was actually only able to take meaningul pictures of 15: the others were usually too frightened or too shy to allow me to photograph them in their normal situations.

Of those I was able to make friends with, however, there was usually a great rapport between us. As I mentioned earlier, if I didn't appear at my regular time, some of the parents would often come out looking for me, or they would delay starting out on their foraging trips until they were sure I was there. At other times they would allow me to accompany them on those hunting expeditions—though I followed at a safe distance so as not to forewarn their prey. Through these experiences I was therefore able to capture on film all aspects of fox-family life.

For me, the foxes were fascinating creatures to observe and study. For them, I was probably a combination of things: a meddlesome neighbor, a whimsical friend, and an overly emotional parent. Through all kinds of weather I was there watching and photographing. It was the familiarity and wàrmth that grew up between us that allowed me to take these pictures. And it was the emotions that I learned then that have made foxes fascinating creatures for me.

The "weathermark" identifies this book as a production of John Weatherhill, Inc., publishers of fine books on Asia and the Pacific. Supervising editor: James T. Conte. Book design and typography: Meredith Weatherby. Production supervisor: Mitsuo Okado. Composition and printing of text, in offset: Komiyama Printing Co., Tokyo. Printing of four-color plates, in offset: Mitsumura Printing Co., Tokyo. Binding: Makoto Binderies, Tokyo. The typeface used is 12-point Monophoto Bembo.